ORATION AGAINST THE TURKS

Pope Pius II
Bishop of Rome

Translated by: D.P. Curtin

Copyright @ 2024 Dalcassian Press LLC

All rights reserved. No part of this publication may be reproduced, distributed, or transmitted in any form or by any means, including photocopying, recording, or other electronic or mechanical methods, without the prior written permission of the publisher, except in the case of brief quotations embodied in critical reviews and certain other non-commercial uses permitted by copyright law. For permission request, write to Dalcassian Press LLC at dalcassianpublishing at gmail.com

ISBN: 979-8-8693-5509-6 (Paperback)

Library of Congress Control Number:
Author: Curtin, D.P. (1985-)

Printed by Ingram Content Group, 1 Ingram Blvd, La Vergne, Tennessee

First printing edition 2024.

ORATION AGAINST THE TURKS

On the following day, the Pontiff addresses the secret consistory advocate and cardinals in this way:

"The sixth year is being passed, men and brothers, after we ascended the chair of the blessed Peter. Meanwhile, which of you has not commended to us the defense of the faith with many great prayers? Who did not say that war should be waged against the Turks and that all the treasures of the Church should be poured out? By your advice and persuasion, we went to Mantua, the Christians, in order to raise the kings, there in a company of war. It did not succeed according to the sentence; the Christians did not listen to the voice of the shepherd. When we returned home, we found everything disturbed.

During that time we saw that almost all of you were trembling with fear, and none of you approved of our plans. You thought that the church would break up, and you could not speak harshly of us who, abandoning the cause of the Turks, had undertaken the French war, and had rather defended the cause of Ferdinand than of Christ.

But what should we do? We would not be able to fight abroad while we were engaged in a domestic war.

Why is this, you ask, such a long story? In order that you may understand the benefits of the great God, with which he has heaped both the Roman Church and you and us, that you may think together with us to repay the turn and to give thanks to the benefactor. The two most serious wars, the Siculus and the Picense, are over, and although some remnants remain in the Kingdom, it is enough that they cannot be a hindrance to our thoughts; Ferdinand himself suffices to remove these small stumbling blocks which remain. We are now free to take up arms against the Turks. We cannot and will not delay any longer. Now we may fulfill our desire, now it is right to fight for the faith that we have always wished for. God knows our thoughts, and he has made the way for them ready at last. You have often asked us to reproached thing; now we will ask you Take care that we may not reproach you for what you reproached for us. Now your faith, your religion, your devotion will come to light. If your charity be true, and not feigned, follow us. We will give you an example, so that, as we ourselves are going to do, you also do. But we will imitate our Master and Lord Jesus Christ, the pious and holy shepherd, who did not hesitate to lay down his life for his sheep. Let us also lay down our lives for our flock, when we cannot otherwise support the Christian religion, lest it be trampled upon by the power of the Turks. We will arm such a fleet as we will be able to equip according to the means of the Church. We will board the ship, although we are old and diseased. We will put sails to the winds and sail to Greece and Asia. And: 'What will you do', someone will say, 'in war, old man? a priest, oppressed by a thousand diseases, and will you go into battle? What will the civilian be able to do in a gang fight? What will the sacred order of cardinals perform in the camp? Hardly will they bring the drums and trumpets, not to mention the bombardments of the enemy. Do you need the youth in the delights, and you will soak the old man with weapons? You act unwisely. You'd better stay at home with the cardinals and all the court. But you will send an army prepared with silver and armed with soldiers accustomed to evils against the enemy, or you will suggest the gold of the Hungarians, who will send the strongest forces possible against the Turks.' Well said and useful, if there is gold. But how can we corroborate it? Our coffers have been exhausted by the long war, and the proceeds of the Church are not sufficient for such a thing, although by the divine gift a vein has been discovered which binds us more and more to divine piety and invites us to protect religion.

We hear your whisperings: 'If you consider war so difficult, with what hope do you proceed if you are not equipped with sufficient forces?' And so we came. A necessary war with the Turks is imminent. Unless we take up arms and meet the enemy, we consider it an act of religion. We shall be such among the Turks as we see among the Jews a despised nation among the Christians. Unless we take war, we are infamous. But war cannot be waged without money. The question arises at this point: where can we find the money? 'By faithful Christians', you will answer. Let us urge further: "By what agreement?" In what way? All avenues have been tried, but no wish has been answered. We mentioned the meeting of Mantua: what fruits emerged from it? We sent ambassadors into the provinces: they were scorned and laughed at. We imposed tithes on the clergy: it was called a pernicious example to the future council. We ordered indulgences to be preached: to say that it was a trap to extort money, and to discover the avarice of the court. Whatever we do, people take it for the worse. Ours is that condition which is that of the stewards' lost faith: nothing is trusted to us; The priesthood is despised, and the name of the clergy is infamous. They say that we act in debauchery, accumulate money, serve ambition, mount mules on fatter and nobler horses, extend the skirts of the swamps, and walk through the city with inflated muzzles under a red cap and a wider hood, feed hounds for hunting, give a lot to actors and parasites, in defense of the faith nothing. Nor do they lie at all: there are most of them among the cardinals and the rest of the curials who do these things, and, if we want to admit the truth, it is too much for our curia either luxury or pride. Hence, we are so hateful to the people that we are not even heard telling the truth.

What do you think should be done in such defiance? Is there not a way to recover lost faith? Of course you say: "And what road will lead us here?' Certainly, none of the usual ones of our times. To cross paths long since unaccustomed. It is necessary to inquire by what arts our forefathers brought forth for us this most extensive dominion of the Church, and to make use of them; for the principality is easily retained by these methods, by which it was born from the beginning. Abstinence, chastity, innocence, zeal for faith. The fervor of religion, the contempt of death, and the desire of martyrdom predominated the Roman church throughout the whole world, the first Peter and Paul falling with inglorious martyrdom. Then followed the pontiffs, one after the other, who were carried away in a long succession to the tribunals of the Gentiles, while they were accusing false gods, and confessing with a clear voice that Christ was the true and unique God, and they agreed to put him to death by elaborate punishments, and with that agreement they consulted the planting of the novel. Let the disciples believe the teachers who spoke the truth, who had confirmed their doctrine with death and could not be torn away from it by any tortures, true and proven shepherds who laid down their lives for their flocks in imitation of Jesus, the eternal and best shepherd, who killed the human race for his sheep on the altar of the cross reconciled to the pious Father Then, when the Romans were converted to Christ, the churches were opened and the gospel spread here and there, the martyrdoms ceased and the holy confessors came in, who by the light of doctrine and the brightness of a holier life benefited the Christian people no less than the martyrs, putting curbs on the vices of men which usually wander more widely in peace. Our church was made great by these and by them. It cannot be preserved unless we imitate our predecessors who founded the kingdom of the church. And it is not enough to be confessors, to preach to the people, to strike down vices, to lift up virtues to heaven: we must approach those earlier who gave up their bodies for the testament of the Lord.

There is nothing that we should not endure for the safety of the flock committed to us, even if the soul is sacrificed.

The Turks are ravaging this and that province of the Christians. Bosna was captured this year and the king of the nation was beheaded. The Hungarians are alarmed, all the neighbors are alarmed. What shall we do? Shall we send armed forces to meet him? You are not the gold from which they are made. What then? Shall we urge the kings to meet them and drive the enemy out of our borders? But this was attempted in vain. It is not well said: go! Perhaps they will listen better: come! I would like to try this. It is a decision to continue the war against the Turks, and to invite the Christian leaders to follow us, both in deed and word. Perhaps when they see their teacher and father, the Roman pontiff, the vicar of Jesus Christ, they will feel sick and sick going to war, they will be ashamed to stay at home; they will take up arms and embrace the defense of the sacred religion with strong souls. If this is not the way to arouse Christians to war, we know of no other. please enter this We know that the situation in our old age is very serious and that we are going to certain death in some way. Nor do we refuse this. We commit all to God. His will be done. We must die at some time, and it does not matter in what place, as long as we die well. Blessed are those who die in obedience to the Lord. A good death redeems a bad life. We shall consider it well done with us, if it please God that our days end in his service. You who have so much encouraged us to make war against the Turks, it is not proper for you to remain at home in idleness: it is necessary to gather your members together with your leader and follow him wherever he goes. What we are doing is of necessity: our departure has been promised to Philip of Burgundy; He had vowed that he would go to war against the Turks, if either the emperor or the king of France, or any other prince whom he did not deign to follow, proposed to do the same. We understood how important Philip's departure was, which was followed by a large part of the West. We desired to begin this journey, and, as they say, to break the ice first, not doubting that a great multitude of nobles and nobles would follow him. ......

Only divine favor is present; the others rushed to victory. Nor do we continue to fight, weak in body and serving as a priesthood, for which it is not proper to wield the sword. Let us imitate that holy father Moses, who prayed on the mountain when Israel was fighting against the Amalekites. We will stand on a high hill or on the brow of a mountain, and having before our eyes the divine Eucharist, that is, our Lord Jesus Christ, we will implore from him salvation and victory for our fighting soldiers. The Lord will not look down upon a broken and humbled heart. You will also be with us, except for the elderly, whom we forgive so that they may remain; and you shall at the same time pray and by good works render propitiation to the divinity of the Christian people. While we say these things, think about it: 'What will be the government of the Roman Church in the meantime? The ultramontanes will refuse to follow you beyond the sea, and in your absence the patrimony of the Church will not be sufficiently safe.' In this way we continue; everything is provided. Listen. We will leave the Roman court and all its offices, and two ambassadors from your order at the city: one will be in charge of spiritual affairs, the other temporal.

In this agreement, as far as we can humanly foresee, we will let everything go in safety. But there is nothing in which we hope more than in the help of the Most High; for unless the lord guards the city, he who guards it watches in vain. For our god we leave our proper seat and the Roman Church and dedicate this gray hair and this weak body to his piety. He will not forget us. If he does not give a return, he will give access to the chamber, and he will keep the first seat and his bride unharmed.

You have heard of our project series. Now you, in turn, promise the opinions of your heart.

While speaking, the pontiff often burst into tears, and neither the cardinals could contain their tears, nor could the cardinals, who were of a sounder mind. The prior in the college who was to answer was the cardinal of Ostia, the priest of the church of Rotomagen, a Frenchman and far removed from the matter proposed, a follower of pleasures and leisure, who did not venture to utter a commanding opinion of the adversary: honesty overcame the nature of man. 'I,' said he, 'and your counsel, pontiff, I praise and admire your spirit. I will follow you wherever you command; although nothing is more difficult for me than the voyage, I will carry whatever burden you impose on me. The Cardinal of Porto, a Spaniard by nationality and an old man, unable to hold back his sobs and tears as they fell, said, 'Up until now I thought you a man, pontiff: now I judge you an angel. You won my opinion. May God be present at your beginnings; I will always be by your side, whether by water or by land, and I will not leave you going through the flames when you are going straight to heaven.' They spoke in almost the same manner as the following to Spoleto, to raise the purpose of the pontiff with the highest praises to heaven.

True, neither the emperor, nor the king of France, nor any other prince superior to him, had the heart to lay arms against the Turks: Philip thought himself freed by his vow, the condition of which had not been fulfilled.

LATIN TEXT

Pontifex sequenti die secretum consistorium advocat cardinalesque hoc modo alloquitur: 'Sextus agitur annus, viri fratres, postquam beati Petri cathedram ascendimus. Quis vestrum interea defensionem fidei non multis magnisque precibus nobis commendavit? Quis non dixit bellum contra Turcum gerendum esse et omnes Ecclesiae thesauros effundendos? Vestro consilio suasuque Mantuam ivimus, christianos ut ibi reges in belli societatem accersiremus. Non successit ex sententia, non audiverunt christiani vocem pastoris. Reuersi domum perturbata omnia reperimus.

Vidimus per id tempus vos ferme omnes trepidare metu nec quisquam vestrum consilia nostra probabat. Ruturam ecclesiam arbitramini nec poteratis de nobis non dura loqui qui re Turcorum obmissa bellum gallicum suscepissemus Ferdinandique magis causam quam Christi defenderemus.

Sed quid ageremus? Occupati bello domestico foris pugnare non poteramus.

Quorsum haec, quaeritis, tam longa narratio? Nempe ut intelligatis beneficia magni dei, quibus et Romanam Ecclesiam et vos nosque cumulavit, ut cogitetis una nobiscum vicem rependere atque habere gratias largitori. Peracta sunt duo gravissima bella, Siculum ac Picense, et quamvis reliquiae in Regno nonnullae remanserint, satis est quod nostris cogitationibus impedimento esse non possunt; ipse per se Ferdinandus minuta haec quae restant evellere offendicula sufficit. Nobis iam liberum est adversus Turcas arma capessere. Non possumus amplius nec volumus differre. Nunc desiderium nostrum implere licet, nunc pro fide pugnare fas est, quod semper optavimus. Novit deus cogitationes nostras hisque viam iam tandem expeditam reddidit. Rogastis nos saepius ut hoc ipsum ageremus; nunc vos rogabimus. Cavete ne, quod in nobis reprehendistis, increpare possimus in vobis. Nunc vestra fides, vestra religio, vestra devotio in lucem veniet. Si vera erit, non ficta caritas vestra, nos sequemini. Exemplum dabimus vobis ut, quemadmodum nos ipsi facturi sumus, ita et vos faciatis. Nos autem magistrum et dominum nostrum Iesum Christum, pium et sanctum pastorem, imitabimur qui pro suis ovibus animam ponere non dubitavit. Ponemus et nos vitam nostram pro grege nostro, quando aliter christianae religioni, ne Turcorum viribus conculcetur, subvenire non possumus. Armabimus classem quantam pro facultatibus Ecclesiae instruere poterimus. Ascendemus navem, quamvis senes morbisque conquassati. Dabimus vela ventis atque in Graeciam et Asiam navigabimus. Et: 'Quid ages', dicet quispiam 'in bello, senex? sacerdos, mille morbis oppressus, et in proelium ibis? Quid togata valebit in pugna cohors? Quid sacer ordo cardinalium praestabit in castris? Vix tympana tubasque ferent, ne dicam bombardas hostium. In delitiis egere iuventam, et tu senium macerabis armis? Inconsulte agis. Melius domi cum cardinalibus atque omni curia remanebis. Classem vero argento paratam fortique et assueto malis milite instructam mittes in hostem aut Hungaris aurum suggeres qui copias quam validissimas in Turcos agant.' Pulchre dictum et utile, si assit aurum. Sed unde id corrademus? Aerarium nostrum diutino bello exhaustum est nec proventus Ecclesiae ii sunt qui tantae rei sufficiant, quamvis divino munere aluminis vena reperta est quae magis ac magis divinae pietati nos obligat et ad tuendam religionem invitat.

Audimus insusurrationes vestras: 'Si adeo difficile bellum censes, qua spe pergis non apparatis viribus quae sufficiant?' Istuc venimus. Bellum necessarium cum Turcis imminet. Nisi sumimus arma atque occurrimus hosti, actum de religione censemus. Tales inter Turcos erimus, qualem inter christianos Iudeorum despectam cernimus gentem. Nisi bellum sumimus, infames sumus. At bellum sine pecunia geri non potest. Quaerere occurrit hoc loco: ubi pecuniam perquiremus? 'A fidelibus christianis', respondebitis. Urgemus amplius: 'Quo pacto?' Quonam modo? Omnes tentatae viae sunt, nulla voto respondit. Indiximus Mantuae conventum: quis inde fructus emersit? Misimus in provincias legatos: spreti atque irrisi fuere. Imposuimus clero decimas: appellatum est pernicioso exemplo ad futurum concilium. Iussimus indulgentias praedicari: aucupium id esse ad extorquendas pecunias dixere et inventum curialis avaritiae. Omnia quaecunque agimus in partem deteriorem populus accipit. Ea conditio nostra est quae mensariorum perdita fide: nihil creditur nobis; despectui sacerdotium est et infame nomen cleri. aiunt nos in delitiis agere, cumulare pecunias, ambitioni servire, mulabus insedere pinguioribus ac nobilioribus equis, extendere fimbrias paludamentorum, et inflatis buccis sub rubente pilleo et ampliori cucullo per Urbem vadere, canes ad venandum alere, histrionibus et parasitis multa largiri, in defensionem fidei nihil. Nec omnino mentiuntur: sunt plerique inter cardinales et reliquos curiales qui haec agunt et, si verum fateri volumus, nimius est curiae nostrae vel luxus vel fastus. Hinc odiosi populo sumus adeo, ut nec vera dicentes audiamur.

Quid agendum in tanta contumacia censetis? An non quaerenda via est qua perditam fidem recuperemus? Utique dicitis: 'Et quae via huc nos ducet?' Nulla certe nostris temporibus usitata. Ad insueta iam pridem itinera transeundum. Quaerendum est quibus artibus maiores nostri hoc nobis imperium Ecclesiae latissimum pepererunt atque illis utendum; principatus enim facile his modis retinetur, quibus ab initio partus est. Abstinentia, castitas, innocentia, zelus fidei. religionis fervor, contemptus mortis martyriique cupido romanam ecclesiam toti orbi prefecerunt, primi Petrus et Paulus inclyto martyrio dicauerunt. Secuti deinde pontifices alter post alterum longa serie ad gentilium tribunalia rapti, dum falsos deos accusant Christumque verum et singularem deum manifesta voce fatentur, exquisitis suppliciis mortem obiere eoque pacto novellae plantationi consuluerunt. Credidere discipuli magistros vera locutos, qui suam doctrinam morte firmassent nec ullis potuerint ab ea tormentis avelli, veri et probati pastores qui pro gregibus suis animam posuerunt magistrum et dominum imitati Iesum, aeternum et optimum pastorem, qui pro suis ovibus in ara crucis occisus humanum genus pio Patri reconciliavit. Conversis deinde ad Christum Romanis, apertis ecclesiis et evangelio passim disseminato, cessavere martyria et sancti confessores introiere, qui doctrinae lumine sanctiorisque vitae fulgore non minus christianis plebibus profuerunt quam martyres, vitiis hominum frena ponentes quae solent in pace latius evagari. Ab his et ab illis ecclesia nostra magna effecta est. Servari non potest, nisi predecessores nostros imitemur qui regnum ecclesiae condidere. Nec satis est confessores esse, praedicare populis, fulminare vitia, virtutes in caelum tollere: ad priores illos accedendum est, qui pro testamento domini sua corpora tradiderunt.

Nihil est quod pro salute gregis nobis commissi perpeti non debeamus, etiam si anima ponenda sit.

Turci modo istam, modo illam christianorum provinciam vastant. Bosna hoc anno capta est et rex gentis obtruncatus. Trepidant Hungari, trepidant vicini omnes. Quid agemus? Armatas illi copias mittemus obviam? Non es aurum unde parentur. Quid ergo? Reges hortabimur illi occurrant qtque hostes e nostris finibus propulsent? At hoc frustra temptatum est. Non belle dicitur: ite! Fortasse melius audient: venite! Hoc temptare libet. Stat sententia in bellum contra Turcas pergere christianosque principes, ut nos sequantur, facto simul et verbis invitare. Fortasse cum viderint magistrum et patrem suum, Romanum pontificem, Jesu Christi vicarium, sentem et aegrotum in bella vadentem, pudebit eos manere domi; arma capient defensionemque sacrae religionis fortibus animis amplectentur. Haec nisi via christianos in bellum excitat, nescimus aliam; hanc ingredi placet. Scimus rem senio nostro pergravem esse nosque ad certam quodammodo mortem profecturos. Neque hanc recusamus. Cuncta deo committimus. Fiat voluntas eius. Moriendum nobis aliquando est, neque interest quo in loco, dum bene moriamur. Beati qui moriuntur in obsequio domini. Mors bona malam vitam redimit. Nobiscum bene actum putabimus, si deo placuerit in eius servitio nostros finiri dies. Vos qui tantopere nos adhortati estis in Turcos movere bellum, domi in otio remanere non decet: oportet membra suo coaptari capiti et illud sequi quocunque ierit. Quod agimus necessitatis est: promissa est profectio nostra Philippo Burgundie duci; votum is voverat profecturum se contra Turcos in bellum, si aut imperator aut rex Franciae aut alius princeps, quem se sequi non dedeceret, idem agere proponeret. Intelligebamus qanti momenti esse profectio Philippi quem magna pars Occidentis sequitur. Cupiebamus hunc iter incipere atque, ut aiunt, glaciem perfringere primum, haud dubitantes quin eum maxima nobilium ac procerum multitudo sectaretur. ......

Adsit tantum divinus favor; ad victoriam cetera succurrrunt. Nec nos pugnaturi pergimus corpore debiles et sacerdotio fungentes, cuius non est proprium versare ferrum. Moysen illum sanctum patrem imitabimur qui pugnante adversus Amalechitas Israhele orabat in monte. Stabimus in alta puppe aut in aliquo montis supercilio habentesque ante oculos divinam eucharistiam, id est dominum nostrum Iesum Christum, ab eo salutem et victoriam pugnantibus nostris militibus implorabimus. Cor contritum et humiliatum non despiciet dominus. Eritis et vos nobiscum exceptis senibus quibus, ut remaneant, ignoscimus; orabitisque pariter et operibus bonis christiano populo divinitatem reddetis propitiam. Cogitatis dum ista dicimus: 'Quod erit interea romanae regimen Ecclesiae? Recusabunt ultramontani ultra mare te sequi nec in absentia tua satis tutum erit Ecclesiae patrimonium.' Istuc pergimus; omnia provisa sunt. Audite. Romanam curiam et omnia eius officia et duos pariter legatos ex ordine vestro apud urbem relinquemus: alter spiritualibus negotiis praeerit, temporalibus alter.

Hoc pacto, quantum humana possumus ratione prospicere, in tuto dimittemus omnia. Sed nihil est in quo magis speremus quam in adiutorio Altissimi; nisi enim dominus custodierit civitatem, frustra vigilat qui custodit eam. Pro deo nostro propriam sedem et romanam Ecclesiam relinquimus et hanc canitiem atque hoc debile corpus suae pietati devovemus. Non erit immemor nostri. Si non dabit reditum, dabit in cealum aditum, et primam sedem sponsamque suam conservabit indemnem.

Audistis propositi nostri seriem. Vos nunc vicissim animi vestri sententias promitte'.

Inter loquendum saepe lacrymatus est pontifex, neque fletum continere cardinales, neque fletum continere cardinales potuerunt, quibus erat mens sanior. Prior in collegio qui responsurus esset cardinalis ostiensis fuit, rhotomagensis ecclesiae pontifex, homo gallicus et a re proposito longe alienus, delitiarum sectator et otii; qui iussus sententiam dicere minime adversari ausus est: naturam hominis rei pervicit honestas. 'Ego', inquit, ' et consilium tuum, pontifex, laudo et animum admiror. Te sequar quocunque iusseris; etsi nihil mihi navigatione difficilius est, onus quodcunque imposueris feram'. Cardinalis portuensis, natione Hispanus atque grandaevus, cadentibus ubertim lacrymis nec singultus retinere valens 'Hominem te', inquit, 'hactenus existimavi, pontifex: nunc angelum iudico. Vicisti opinionem meam. Deus adsit tuis coeptis; ego lateri tuo semper comes adero sive aqua sive terra sit iter habendum, nec te per flammas euntem deseram quando recta in caelum vadis.' Similia fere locuti sequentes ad Spoletanum usque pontificis propositum summis in caelum laudibus extulere.

Verum neque imperator neque rex Franciae neque princeps alius eo superior in Turcos poferre arma apposuit animum: solutum se voto Philippus existimabat, cuius non esset impleta conditio.

The Scriptorium Project is the work of a small group of lay people of various apostolic churches who are interested in the preservation, transmission, and translation of the works of the early and medieval church. Our efforts are to make the works of the church fathers accessible to anyone who might have an interest in Christian antiquities and the theological, philosophical, and moral writings that have become the bedrock of Western Civilization.

To-date, our releases have pulled from the Greek, Nordic, Visigothic, Slavic, Armenian, Syriac, Georgian, Anglo-Saxon, Byzantine, Persian, German, Celtic, Ethiopian, and Coptic traditions of Christianity, and have been pulled from sundry local traditions and languages.

www.ingramcontent.com/pod-product-compliance
Lightning Source LLC
LaVergne TN
LVHW061044070526
838201LV00073B/5175